VERSUS

COKE vs PEPSI
THE COLA WARS

KENNY ABDO

Fly!
An Imprint of Abdo Zoom
abdobooks.com

abdobooks.com

Published by Abdo Zoom, a division of ABDO, P.O. Box 398166, Minneapolis, Minnesota 55439. Copyright © 2023 by Abdo Consulting Group, Inc. International copyrights reserved in all countries. No part of this book may be reproduced in any form without written permission from the publisher. Fly!™ is a trademark and logo of Abdo Zoom.

Printed in the United States of America, North Mankato, Minnesota.
102022
012023

Photo Credits: Alamy, flickr, Getty Images, Shutterstock,
©Gerry Dincher p.10/ CC BY-SA 2.0
Production Contributors: Kenny Abdo, Jennie Forsberg, Grace Hansen
Design Contributors: Candice Keimig, Neil Klinepier, Laura Graphenteen

Library of Congress Control Number: 2021950283

Publisher's Cataloging-in-Publication Data

Names: Abdo, Kenny, author.
Title: Coke vs. Pepsi: the cola wars / by Kenny Abdo.
Other title: the cola wars
Description: Minneapolis, Minnesota : Abdo Zoom, 2023 | Series: Versus |
    Includes online resources and index.
Identifiers: ISBN 9781098228620 (lib. bdg.) | ISBN 9781098229467 (ebook) |
    ISBN 9781098229887 (Read-to-Me ebook)
Subjects: LCSH: Coca-Cola Company--Juvenile literature. | Pepsi-Cola Company-
    Juvenile literature. | Soda industry--Juvenile literature. | Competition-
    Economic aspects--Juvenile literature.
Classification: DDC 338.7--dc23

TABLE OF CONTENTS

Coke vs. Pepsi.................... 4

The Companies................... 8

Fight! 14

Legacy 18

Glossary 22

Online Resources 23

Index 24

COKE VS PEPSI

The Coca-Cola Company and PepsiCo, Inc. have been in a century-long rivalry that has blown the lid off the industry! It is known as "the cola wars."

The cola wars mainly took place in the mid-1970s and '80s. And it was a fizzy battle to **dominate** the soft drink market.

THE COMPANIES

Coca-Cola was invented in 1886 by **pharmacist** John S. Pemberton. He soon began selling the sugary drink to **soda fountains**.

Six years later, the Coca-Cola Company was founded.

Pepsi was invented by **pharmacist** Caleb Bradham in 1893. Five years later, he changed the name from "Brad's Drink" to "Pepsi-Cola." The Pepsi-Cola Company was founded in 1902.

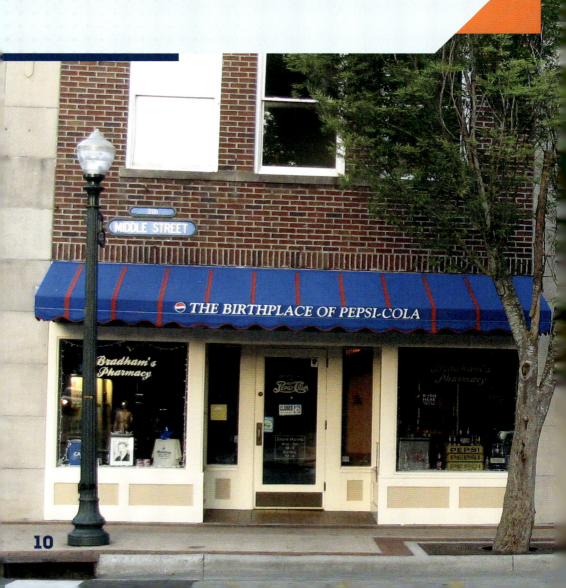

For decades, Coke was more popular than Pepsi. Eventually, the companies began taking aim at each other through marketing **campaigns**.

FIGHT!

The cola wars began heating up in 1975. Pepsi launched a **campaign** called the Pepsi Challenge. It showed blind taste tests where more people chose Pepsi over Coke.

In 1985, Coca-Cola launched New Coke. Customers were upset, wanting the original. Pepsi took advantage of the **backlash**. They claimed their soda was "the choice of a new generation." Pepsi got several celebrities to promote the soda, like Michael Jackson and Britney Spears!

Coca-Cola relaunched its original soda as Coca-Cola Classic just three months after the New Coke **fiasco**. The company also released popular new recipes like Cherry Coke.

In 2010, Diet Coke sales topped Pepsi for the first time. It became the second-most popular soft drink in the U.S. *The Wall Street Journal* ran the headline, "Diet Coke Wins Battle in Cola Wars."

LEGACY

18

Coca-Cola is sold in every country in the world except for two. The commercial, "I'd Like to Buy the World a Coke," is considered one of the most popular ads of all time.

Pepsi **merged** with Frito Lay in the mid-60s to create PepsiCo. Though the soda may not sell as much as Coke, its snack food business is enormous.

Coca-Cola sales have beat Pepsi's for years. Yet the two sodas are consistently the top two best-sellers. The victor of the cola wars could change at the pop of a can.

GLOSSARY

backlash – a strong reaction against something.

campaign – a series of planned actions done to reach a particular goal like selling a product.

dominate – to have control over something.

fiasco – an enormous failure. Usually seen as a disaster.

merge – to combine two or more companies into one business.

pharmacist – a person licensed to prepare and sell medicine.

soda fountains – a device used to dispense soft drinks like Pepsi and Coke.

ONLINE RESOURCES

To learn more about Coke and Pepsi, please visit **abdobooklinks.com** or scan this QR code. These links are routinely monitored and updated to provide the most current information available.

INDEX

Bradham, Caleb 10

campaigns 14, 15, 19

Cherry Coke 16

Cola Wars 7, 12, 17, 21

Diet Coke 17

Frito Lay (company) 20

Jackson, Michael 15

New Coke 15, 16

Pemberton, John S. 8

Spears, Britney 15

Wall Street Journal (newspaper) 17